NEW YORK CITY'S
ITALIAN
NEIGHBORHOODS

Devotees within the Two Bridges neighborhood flock the statue of St. Rocco, which has been processed throughout the former Italian neighborhood since 1889. (Author's collection.)

FRONT COVER (clockwise from left): In Williamsburg, children participate in the Dance of the Giglio in honor of San Paolino di Nola. (Author's collection; see page 61.) On a Vespa, a couple crosses the famous intersection of Grand and Mulberry Streets. (Author's collection; see page 20.) Caffe Capri has been on Graham Avenue (also known as Via Vespucci) in Williamsburg, Brooklyn, since 1974. (Author's collection; see page 59.)

UPPER BACK COVER: The St. Anthony's Bakery in Dyker Heights, Brooklyn, has been churning out some of the best Italian bread and cookies in the five boroughs for decades. Owned by the same family since inception, the old-fashioned bakery prides itself on the most delicious seven-layered cookies, semolina bread, bread sticks, and many more classic Italian baked goods. (Author's collection; see page 27.)

LOWER BACK COVER (from left to right): A local gentleman sits on his stoop to get some fresh air in East Williamsburg. (Author's collection; see page 60.) Devotion, passion, and love emanate from the open arms of Stephen LaRocca, the president of the St. Rocco Society of Potenza, as he shouts, "Viva San Rocco," while society members carry the statue of St. Rocco down the steps of the 128-year-old Shrine Church of the Most Precious Blood in Manhattan's famed Little Italy. (Author's collection; see page 15.) Featured in many movies and television shows, the 120-year-old Veniero's Pasticceria not only still serves the East Village neighborhood of Manhattan, but also ships its famously delicious pastries all over the United States. (Author's collection; see page 26.)

NEW YORK CITY'S ITALIAN NEIGHBORHOODS

Raymond Guarini with
Cav. John Napoli

ARCADIA
PUBLISHING

Copyright © 2019 by Raymond Guarini with Cav. John Napoli
ISBN 9781540241276

Published by Arcadia Publishing
Charleston, South Carolina

Library of Congress Control Number: 2019943331

For all general information, please contact Arcadia Publishing:
Telephone 843-853-2070
Fax 843-853-0044
E-mail sales@arcadiapublishing.com
For customer service and orders:
Toll-Free 1-888-313-2665

Visit us on the Internet at www.arcadiapublishing.com

*I am dedicating this book to my family for being my
motivation, especially my inspiring son and my father
for instilling such a strong pride of our heritage.*

CONTENTS

Acknowledgments   6

Introduction   7

1.   Little Italy and Manhattan's Other Italian Neighborhoods   9

2.   Brooklyn's Popular and Lesser-Known
     Little Italy Neighborhoods   27

3.   The Italian Sections of Queens   65

4.   The Bronx's Famed Little Italy and Villa Avenue   77

About the Italian Enclaves Historical Society   95

ACKNOWLEDGMENTS

I thank John Napoli, of the blog *Il Regno: Altar and Throne*, for his valued friendship; he eagerly donated many photographs for the creation of this book. Special thanks go to the men and women of the St. Rocco Society of Potenza for their unparalleled devotion in 130 years of continuing Southern Italian customs and to society president, Stephen LaRocca, for his contagious passion. I also thank the Italian American business owners, Giglio lifters and bands, and clergy who support the continuation of Italian American customs. Many thanks are given to the social media followers of Italian Enclaves and to the supporters of the Italian Enclaves Historical Society for providing positive feedback and whose continued interaction and support makes my work of passion so much more enjoyable. Unless otherwise specified, all images appear courtesy of the author's collection.

INTRODUCTION

Over four million Italians arrived in the United States by 1920 via Ellis Island. Many of them settled nearby in the five boroughs of New York City: the Bronx, Brooklyn, Queens, Staten Island, and Manhattan. Within each borough, there were many Italian neighborhoods that have existed at some point since the beginning of the Italian migration in the 1870s, and some still remain. Documenting these neighborhoods is no easy task as New York City's five boroughs comprise such a massive amount of space.

This book endeavors not only to educate readers as to which Italian neighborhoods have existed and still exist, but to also capture the essence of these neighborhoods by showcasing their hearts and souls: the businesses, churches, and events that are the cornerstones of Italian American culture in New York City's five boroughs. Many Italian neighborhoods in New York City only have remnants of what were once thriving enclaves while some still have many Italians living in them, and yet others maintain no signs of their former settlers whatsoever.

From the character of Italian storefronts to the devotion of the Dance of the Giglio in both Harlem and Williamsburg, this book serves to highlight the unparalleled pride and devotion maintained by the Italian American community in New York City.

As events like World War I and World War II reshaped Europe, Italians (particularly from Southern Italy) were forced to find new homes across the Atlantic where the unparalleled opportunity existed to practice sovereign freedoms such as maintaining exhibitions of faith as well as pursuing trades and, eventually, professions.

As settlers arrived in New York City via Ellis Island, prosperity became tangible by virtue of the industrial revolution and the need for jobs such as longshoremen, factory workers, and skilled labor, like stonemasons, bricklayers, and artists. Following family members across the Atlantic and into New York City, Italians began congregating into enclaves that were reconstructions of the towns from which they emigrated. Once in their new towns within the five boroughs, Italian immigrants began to open pork stores, fish markets, bakeries, and eateries to meet the demand for familiarity within their new land. Many of these businesses are still open today and have proudly been passed from one generation to another.

What is phenomenal about the Italian immigrants was their religious devotion. Having first been forced to practice their religion in the basements of other Catholic churches and unfamiliar with the language, the Italians petitioned the Archdiocese of New York for their own churches. They were given authority to build their own parishes, which were referred to as national parishes due to their being opened to specifically celebrate Mass in the language of the parishioners. Italian national parishes were often constructed by the very immigrants for whom they were being built. In some cases, such as the Church of Our Lady of Mount Carmel in East Harlem, these churches were built entirely at night with no light but candlelight and the moon to illuminate their work. Unparalleled in talent, Italian stonemasons worked tirelessly into the wee hours after having worked entire days. The masons, carpenters, and artists harnessed every scrap they could find in order to construct their places of worship to resemble the churches in their hometowns in Italy. In many cases, statues of saints were either shipped over to the United States from Italy or were carved in New York from scratch out of wood or chiseled out of stone.

As the populations aged in Italian neighborhoods, the need for funeral parlors became apparent. A business very close to their religion due to the sanctity of the funeral Mass, Italians became some of the most talented and well-renowned funeral directors in America.

Italians were not very reliant at all on the government for help. There were few to no social programs in place during the early arrivals of Italian immigrants, so the Italian people created mutual aid societies to help one another support their families in times of need or in the event of the loss of a loved one. Such things that the mutual aid societies helped finance were medical expenses, funeral expenses, and a form of life insurance. In addition, they were the starting point of sponsorship networks whereby Italian immigrants could find a sponsor in accordance with US immigration policy at the time. Without a sponsorship providing a job and a home, no one could come into the country. These mutual aid societies are shown throughout this book and are still in existence in almost every Italian neighborhood in New York City; however, their functions today are more religious and social.

The Italian neighborhoods shifted and migrated within the five boroughs throughout the decades. The growth of the subway and modern modes of transportation enabled Italians to spread from Manhattan to the other boroughs at the turn of the 20th century just as the building of highways would displace constituents throughout the boroughs. The last major diasporic shift of Italians within New York City occurred when the Verrazzano Bridge was built, thus enabling Italians in different parts of New York to move into the more suburban Staten Island.

One

LITTLE ITALY AND MANHATTAN'S OTHER ITALIAN NEIGHBORHOODS

In East Harlem, the annual feast of il Giglio di Sant' Antonio (St. Anthony) is under way. Here, outside the Church of Our Lady of Mount Carmel, the Giglio Band performs atop a platform being carried on the shoulders of men. Manhattan has had many Italian neighborhoods since the 1870s. Despite many of these neighborhoods completely dismantling as early as the mid-20th century, there are some strong visual remnants of the Italian neighborhoods of Manhattan.

The statue of St. Anthony of Padua is holding the Christ Child and *giglios* (lilies), which represent purity, innocence, and integrity. It is common for believers to place lilies in one hand of a St. Anthony statue and pray for his intercession. Here, money is attached to the saint as a tribute to the church and Giglio Society of East Harlem to properly maintain the event's authenticity. Having originated in Italy, this celebration was brought by immigrants to the United States over 100 years ago.

The famed Claudio's Barbershop is located on 116th Street; its proprietor and barber, Claudio, has been cutting hair for 60 years. His clientele not only includes average citizens, but also politicians, actors, and famous entertainers.

Il Giglio stands proudly on Pleasant Avenue and 118th Street. Note its ornate craftsmanship and beautiful depictions of St. Anthony. The Giglio Society is one huge family weaved together across generations of this East Harlem neighborhood. Frankie Bracco was announced as 2017's No. 1 *capo paranza* (chief lifter).

Pictured is an East Harlem landmark, Patsy's, located on First Avenue between 118th and 117th Streets. In the same spot since the neighborhood's original Italian population lived there, the pizzeria is still drawing crowds from near and far.

As the procession of Sant' Antonio is about to start, current and former neighbors reconvene and catch up on the stoop across from the Church of Our Lady of Mount Carmel.

At the time of this photograph, Marrone Bakery was already out of business, but the beloved bakery had been thriving for decades. It drew customers from around the country, including Frank Sinatra. Rosa Marrone, a neighborhood backbone, was a staunch supporter of the Sant' Antonio feast.

The Giglio stands proudly in front of the heart of the East Harlem Italian community, the Church of Our Lady of Mount Carmel. A young girl holds one of the ropes that keeps the Giglio sturdy.

Pictured are parishioners and members of the East Harlem Giglio Society celebrating Mass at the Church of Our Lady of Mount Carmel prior to the start of the annual feast of il Giglio di Sant' Antonio.

On Pleasant Avenue and East 118th Street, Rao's, a neighborhood holdover and internationally known phenomenon, is still serving patrons who are lucky enough to get a seat at one of its tables. Reservations are not possible at this close-knit iconic eatery. One must be invited by someone who owns a table.

Stephen LaRocca, president of the St. Rocco Society of Potenza, passionately yells, "Viva San Rocco," as he places a gold necklace around the saint statue as a sign of adoration. This saint procession, held on the opposite side of Manhattan in the Two Bridges neighborhood, was first hosted by San Joachim Church and then, after San Joachim was demolished, by the Church of San Giuseppe on Catherine Street. Since the closure of San Giuseppe, the feast and procession are now sponsored by the Shrine Church of the Most Precious Blood on Baxter Street.

A very important part of Italian culture is to carry on certain religious services, such as wakes and funeral Masses, so that the families of the departed can have loved ones, friends, and community members show their respect and support. Italian funeral homes have become quite legendary institutions in their own right within Italian neighborhoods. This photograph depicts the 2018 closure of Vanella's Funeral Chapel in the Two Bridges neighborhood, a reflection of the demographic shifts that have occurred in Manhattan.

At the 129th annual celebration of the feast of St. Rocco, the saint statue is carried out of the Shrine Church of the Most Precious Blood to welcoming cheers of joy and bursts of confetti. Stephen LaRocca emphatically raises his arms to welcome the beloved saint. (Courtesy of Joseph Lucia.)

The Red Mike Festival Band proudly marches along Mulberry Street and plays for a whopping crowd that reaches into the millions throughout the entire course of the San Gennaro feast.

As the sign says, Piemonte Ravioli Co., Inc., was established in 1920. This type of storefront was once commonplace in the Italian neighborhood of Little Italy, which surrounds Mulberry Street, but today, fewer remain with the character exhibited by Piemonte.

A living legend, Ernesto Rossi, of E. Rossi & Co., Inc., showcases the flag of Two Sicilies in his 100-year-old Italian novelty shop. Ernesto, or "Ernie" for those who know him, is being visited by Prince Charles of Bourbon–Two Sicilies, Duke of Castro.

Members of the San Gennaro Society, the Knights of the Constantinian Military Order of St. George, and various Italian American dignitaries and cultural preservationists pose for a photograph in front of the statue of San Gennaro during the 2018 feast day.

The beautifully adorned St. Anthony and Infant Jesus statues are being processed in downtown Little Italy. Devotions for St. Anthony are very common among Italian communities in the five boroughs. Every detail of the statue is noteworthy, like the clothing, which was specially made for the statue; the crown of baby Jesus; the money pinned to the saint; and the floral arrangement.

Dressed in religiously and culturally significant garb, children are also part of the festivities as they process with the saint.

Here, a different St. Anthony statue is being processed along Mulberry Street. This statue is also flanked by flowers and held atop the shoulders of devotees and society members.

Vincent's, one of the oldest Italian restaurants in New York City's five boroughs, is located at the corner of 119th and Mott Streets. The Chinese signage in the photograph captures the essence of the dwindling Little Italy and encroaching Chinatown.

Due to the burgeoning numbers of Italians in the early 20th century, the Church of the Most Holy Crucifix was built in 1925 to serve Little Italy. Located at 378 Broome Street, the church is referred to as the Chapel of San Lorenzo Ruiz today.

A couple zips through the crowded streets of Little Italy on their Vespa. Pictured in the background is the famed Alleva cheese store, as well as Ferrarra Pastry Shop and E. Rossi & Co.

As the sign says, the "oldest cheese store in America, est. 1892," Alleva is still serving some of the country's best mozzarella and ricotta, among other Italian foods. Around 2014, famous actor Tony Danza became an investor and partner in Alleva.

Piemonte Ravioli Co., Inc., mentioned earlier, still maintains a retail shop for either the loyal customers who have moved but still return for its products or the newcomers who wish to try New York City's best-of-the-best Italian food shops.

DiPalo's Fine Foods, established in 1925, is a world-famous Italian food source in Little Italy at 200 Grand Street, Manhattan. Frequently, owner Lou DiPalo is featured on television or in print for his vast knowledge of Italian food.

A view uptown along Mulberry Street shows tourists and pedestrians traversing Little Italy's row of restaurants, namely Café Napoli, which is still there serving some of Manhattan's best fare.

On the grounds of the recently sold rectory of the Shrine Church of the Most Precious Blood on Mulberry Street, this now-gone war memorial lists the names of the fallen men from the Little Italy neighborhood stemming back to World War I up until, most recently, the wars in the Middle East. For a full list of names, please see the Italian Enclaves Historical Society website at www.italianenclaves.com.

Also on the grounds of the recently sold rectory of the Shrine Church of the Most Precious Blood on Mulberry Street, this garden of statues reflects Italian Americans' devotion to SS. Anthony, Padre Pio, Our Lady of Guadalupe, and Francis of Assisi.

Society members begin the procession of St. Anthony out of the Shrine Church of the Most Precious Blood on Baxter Street.

A lost art and sight, a minstrel serenades onlookers and diners at the sidewalk eateries along Mulberry Street.

As the procession of St. Rocco weaves through Little Italy, Chinatown, and the old Two Bridges neighborhood, the statue starts to make its way back to the Shrine Church of the Most Precious Blood with a sea of devotees.

Hopping to the Lower East Side, about two miles north of Little Italy, there are still remnants of the Italian neighborhood that once comprised about two square miles of Manhattan tenements, such as this Peter Jarema Funeral Home.

Also in the Lower East Side neighborhood, a fixture since 1894, Veniero's Pasticceria (left) is still serving some of New York's finest Italian pastry. A favorite of Frank Sinatra when he was in town, Veniero's draws tourists and celebrity clientele alike. Located at 168 First Avenue in the East Village, Lanza's (right) was a legendary Italian restaurant and lasted for about 100 years. The eatery closed its doors in 2017 and was reinvented as Joe & Pat's. The classic stained-glass window moniker still exists.

The Lower East Side neighborhood's famed Russo's, where fresh mozzarella and ricotta made it famous, still has customers coming in from all over town.

Two

Brooklyn's Popular and Lesser-Known Little Italy Neighborhoods

One of the last holdovers on this strip along Fort Hamilton Parkway, St. Anthony's Bakery in Brooklyn has been making the finest Italian bread and cookies for decades. The zip code technically places this bakery within Borough Park, but it is unquestionably within the confines of Dyker Heights and is sometimes also considered a part of Bay Ridge.

An Italian national parish, St. Bernadette, was first established in 1935, and before this attractive church and grounds were created, parishioners worshipped in a storefront at 8218 Thirteenth Avenue. This is the Shrine Church of St. Bernadette.

The grotto outside the shrine is replete with running water, a statuary, and votive candles. The names of parishioners are on the stone tiles surrounding the font.

Located at 7714 Eighteenth Avenue, the heart of Bensonhurst, Tribuzio and Cottone's classic signage and storefront signify an enduring appreciation for the old-world butcher shop.

Here, members of a younger generation are introduced to the sacred traditions held by their families as devotees draw a cart carrying the statue of St. Anthony through the streets of Bath Beach, in Brooklyn. Blessed bread is also drawn in tow and handed to people standing along the sidewalks as donations are pinned to the saint in return for special graces and intentions.

The once ubiquitous social club has always been the cornerstone of Italian neighborhoods. First formed as mutual aid societies to provide insurance for member families, this particular society, the Caduti Superga Mola Soccer Club, whose members are from Mola in Bari, show their devotion to St. Padre Pio by processing the statue of the saint from its clubhouse in Bensonhurst, Brooklyn.

On Good Friday, many Italian neighborhoods pay homage to Our Lady of Sorrows by processing a solemn-faced statue of the Blessed Mother dressed in black and gold. The men wear tuxedos as black symbolizes the mourning of the death of Jesus. This procession is beginning from the steps of St. Athanasius Church in Bensonhurst, Brooklyn.

Established in 1902 as an Italian national parish, St. Rosalia Church on Fourteenth Avenue and Sixty-third Street has since been demolished but served as a centerpiece for its Dyker Heights community.

Yard statues and shrines have always been a unique characteristic of Italian neighborhoods. This decades-old shrine to St. Anthony is still proudly standing in a front yard on a side street in Bensonhurst, Brooklyn.

During Good Friday, as the procession passes by hundreds of homes in Bensonhurst, yard shrines are made along the procession route and elsewhere throughout the neighborhood in honor of Our Lady of Sorrows.

For decades, the feast of St. Rosalia, the patroness of Sicily, spanned as far as the eye could see. Now, the feast runs from Sixty-fifth Street to Seventy-fifth Street but was once 10 blocks longer. As the neighborhood demographics have changed, the feast is now more multicultural and welcomes people of all backgrounds to enjoy Italian delicacies.

Italian barbershops have always been held dear in the hearts of New Yorkers, and that has not changed as this more-recent and modern barbershop on Eighteenth Avenue proudly adorns the Italian flag along with the American flag.

Multifamily brick row homes are a common sight in the five boroughs. Most were built between the turn of the century and the 1920s. These classic-looking row houses maintain charming tin awnings, as well as a St. Anthony yard statue.

Italian pride is common throughout Bensonhurst, Brooklyn, but there is also American pride. The fact that United States has provided the Italian community with so many amazing opportunities is not lost on the owners of this home; the flag incorporates both those of Italy and the United States. Note the St. Jude statue outside this family's home.

Along the heart of Bensonhurst, Eighteenth Avenue, an Italian eatery and catering business, La Cucina, proudly represents its heritage with an Italian flag, accompanied by an American flag, outside.

Here is another example of a yard shrine in Bensonhurst. This shrine, made of steel, siding, and Plexiglas, encases statues of the Sacred Heart of Jesus and SS. Anthony and Joseph.

Moving across Brooklyn from Bensonhurst to Bergen Beach, the feast of Our Lady of Carmel is under way in front of St. Bernard Church. This small neighborhood feast is two blocks long but draws many Italians from Bergen Beach and the surrounding areas of Flatlands and Mill Basin. Members of the Giosa Marina Society dutifully guard and help dress the statue with ribbons and flowers as votive candles are sold for intentions.

Here is another look at the festivities at St. Bernard Church in Bergen Beach, Brooklyn, hosted by the Gioiosa Marina Social Club. The St. Anthony statue indicates the strong devotion that Southern Italians maintain in this part of Brooklyn. People prepare gifts to be sold under the church's canopy to raise money for the society and church.

This photograph, taken looking down East Sixty-ninth Street from Avenue U, shows a breathtaking sunset with a Ferris wheel and feast lights decorating the summer night's landscape.

The legendary Circo's Pastry Shop is virtually the last remnant of a very Sicilian neighborhood along Knickerbocker Avenue, in the Bushwick section of Brooklyn. Hart Street and Knickerbocker Avenue were at the heart of this Sicilian neighborhood, which dispersed in the 1980s.

This cross street marks the center of the one- and two-family homes that comprised the residential base of Italian Bushwick. Ann Maggio Way was named in honor of a local resident who was committed to her neighbors. Originally from Ridgewood, Maggio moved to Suydam Street in 1939. She was an activist and helped found the Suydam Street Block Association in 1985.

As stated earlier, the Italian churches were and still are the heart and soul of every Italian community. Bushwick was no exception, as St. Joseph Patron, whose rectory and beautiful Sacred Heart of Jesus statue, exemplifies the strong devotional prowess of this one-time Italian neighborhood.

While Bushwick transitioned many decades ago, there are still signs within the residential neighborhood that indicate either current or former Italian presence, such as this Blessed Mother statue in the yard of a home on Hart Street.

Frances Cabrini was a member of the Missionary Sisters of the Sacred Heart of Jesus. She came to America and founded numerous hospitals, orphanages, and schools. As one can see here, this school on Suydam Street was named after her for her saintly work in educating Italian immigrant children.

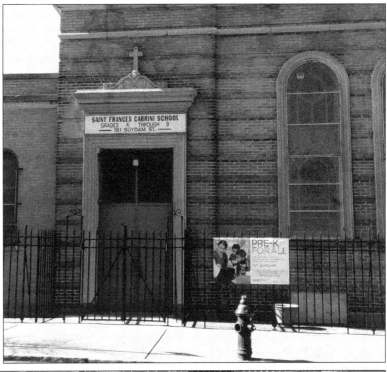

In Canarsie, Brooklyn, there was a thriving Italian neighborhood that, just like Bushwick, has long dissipated. Sonny's, however, is still turning out some of the best Italian hero sandwiches in the five boroughs.

Guarino Funeral Home, located at 9222 Flatlands Avenue, is a Canarsie institution. Many residents who have left the neighborhood still return to have their family members' funeral services here. Again, a common theme in Italian neighborhoods, the funeral home plays a very special role in community cohesiveness.

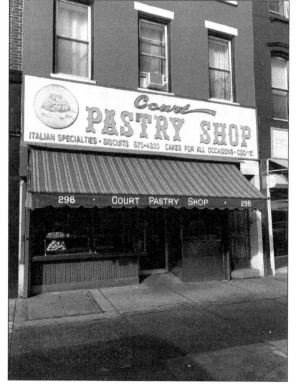

In Carroll Gardens, Brooklyn, a staple among residents is the Court Pastry Shop. Located at 298 Court Street, Court Pastry has been in business for over 50 years. Having first been settled at the end of the 1800s, Carroll Gardens is a very old Italian neighborhood and still maintains a lot of Italian residents.

In Carroll Gardens, a neighborhood made famous for the sprawling front gardens of striking turn-of-the-century brownstones, there is a Sicilian trinacria floral arrangement, possibly from a family member's funeral.

Here is a beautiful bronze statue of St. Anthony in a well-manicured front yard in Carroll Gardens.

This is another prime example of a handsome brownstone with a yard statue of the Blessed Mother in Carroll Gardens, Brooklyn.

Along Henry Street in Carroll Gardens, Brooklyn, there are still a few social clubs for Italian mutual aid societies. This extremely interesting storefront sports a members-only sign and a St. Anthony statue.

Pictured is the facade of the recently closed Raccuglia Funeral Home on the corner of Court and Sackett Streets in Carroll Gardens, Brooklyn. The place where many Italian Americans, throughout the entire city, would have their family services, Raccuglia proudly displays devotion to Mother Cabrini as seen in the stained-glass window in front.

As this Sacred Heart of Jesus statue exemplifies, yard statues in Carroll Gardens are among the most ornate in the city. Adorned for Christmastime, lights accentuate the beauty of this resident's devotion.

Along Court Street, the main street of Carroll Gardens, an Italian restaurant that is somewhat of a time capsule still exists and is called Sam's. The storefront evokes a character reminiscent of a time long gone, and the service, food, and atmosphere remain the same.

A mainstay of Carroll Gardens, Ferdinando's Focacceria represents the Sicilian influence in the Italian culture within the neighborhood. Known for its signature panelle special and Manhattan special espresso on tap, Ferdinando's is a delectable taste of old school in a rapidly gentrifying neighborhood.

Yet another devotional centerpiece, this crowned Blessed Mother statue, surrounded by flowers, is on display in a lovely front garden in Carroll Gardens.

The devotions to different saints among Italians could not be more evident than in this photograph. In front of one home, a Padre Pio statue stands proudly, while the next yard over maintains the more common statue of the Virgin Mary.

Two Italian women stroll down Henry Street and catch up on the goings-on in the Carroll Gardens neighborhood. Enfolded in a classic scene, they meander past lush gardens with red tin canopies in the background, which give an Italianesque feel to this photograph.

What is an Italian neighborhood without a pork store? G. Esposito & Sons at 357 Court Street in Carroll Gardens, Brooklyn, has been around since 1922 and is a neighborhood institution. The pig statue just adds to the character of the neighborhood.

The Barese make up a good portion of the Italians in Carroll Gardens, Brooklyn. The Van Westerhout Cittadini Cultural & Social Club is a neighborhood fixture that welcomes people with open arms to take part in its many celebrations with delicious delicacies.

Just next to Carroll Gardens is the old neighborhood Gowanus. It is now mostly industrial and commercial but still has remnants of a significant Italian community that has lived here since the late 1800s. This residence prides itself with a quaint porch and encased Blessed Mother statue.

Gowanus still has a handful of Italian residents, and many still return to fraternize at the Glory Social Club on Third Avenue. The club has always been home to wonderful holiday parties for Christmas, the Fourth of July, and so on.

Our Lady of Sorrows, or better known among the local community as Maria SS. Addolorata, has a very strong devotion among the Carroll Gardens community and is processed each year from Sacred Hearts Jesus and Mary and St. Stephen Church (pictured), located on the corner of Hicks and Summit Streets.

A picture is worth a thousand words. In this home set back from the sidewalk in Bath Beach, Brooklyn, an Our Lady of Mount Carmel statue still proudly stands but withered by age. A for sale sign, which is much more common in these parts nowadays, foretells the changing of the guard in Bath Beach's Italian community.

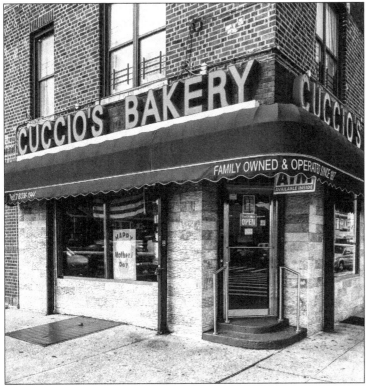

Next to Bath Beach is another neighborhood called Gravesend, which has historically been lumped together with Bensonhurst but is distinctly its own neighborhood. Cuccio's bakery is a family-owned and -operated institution.

The Gioiosa Marina Social Club, named after the town from which most of its members derived, is located at 2378 Flatbush Avenue in the Marine Park section of Brooklyn.

The Pastosa Meat Market is located in what is referred to as Old Mill Basin, near the Flatlands section of eastern Brooklyn. This neighborhood was once home to a thriving Italian community as early as the early 20th century.

Pastosa Ravioli is a legendary business with multiple locations throughout the five boroughs and other parts of New York. This location in Old Mill Basin, on East Fifty-third Street and Avenue N, draws people back to their old neighborhood as well as patrons from Marine Park, Mill Basin, and Bergen Beach.

Established in 1985, La Torre Pork Store, which recently changed hands, still stands and serves delicious Italian delicacies right off Flatbush Avenue on Avenue N in the Marine Park/Old Mill Basin section of Brooklyn.

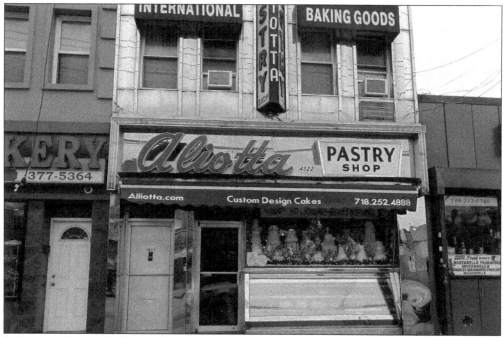

Right next door to La Torre, Aliotta Pastry Shop has been around for decades. Supplying many restaurants and caterers with cakes, the shop is one of the most renowned Italian bakeries in the five boroughs.

On Flatbush Avenue, Torregrossa & Sons Funeral Home provides local families the opportunity to grieve for their loved ones in a beautiful setting. Torregrossa has two other locations in Brooklyn.

In Sunset Park, Brooklyn, there was a small pocket of Italians. Luigi's Pizza and its classic signage are vestiges of that old neighborhood. Particularly interesting is the aged brick in this turn-of-the-century building.

A row home in Sunset Park proudly exhibits a Sacred Heart statue either from a current Italian resident or leftover from a former one.

St. Rocco's Roman Catholic Church in Sunset Park, Brooklyn, is an Italian national parish built by and for Italian immigrants residing in the area. This Italian neighborhood, which was about five blocks by two blocks long, was centered around this church.

Although the signage remains and the storefront still looks original, this Pasticceria has recently been sold by the original owners. The new proprietors wanted to keep things the same so not to disturb the character of the bakery.

Many of the homes in Sunset Park are either brownstone or sandstone row houses, which are highly desirable pieces of real estate for new homeowners who often renovate or restore these properties. This photograph shows a St. Francis of Assisi statue, with a pigeon coincidentally flying above, at what was once or still is an Italian family's home.

Williamsburg, Brooklyn, was one of the first Italian neighborhoods in the five boroughs. As Italians moved from the early settlements of Manhattan in search of work in the burgeoning borough of Brooklyn, they needed a place of worship, so St. Anthony of Padua was built.

On the corner of Ainslie and Leonard Streets in the East Williamsburg Italian neighborhood, an elaborate encased yard shrine to the Blessed Mother can be seen here.

The Giglio Boys of Williamsburg's clubhouse dons the Italian and US flags and a sign from its feast, which showcases a congratulatory announcement. This club is open to anyone who is devoted. There is a children's Giglio as well.

This street in East Williamsburg, Brooklyn, displays the neighborhood's Italian pride, and if one looks carefully, a statue of San Paolino can be seen in the front yard to the left. Note the Italian flag painted on the fire hydrant and mailbox off in the distance.

Located on Graham Avenue (Via Vespucci), the main artery of East Williamsburg's Italian neighborhood, the now-closed Grande Monuments store supplied the neighborhood with yard statues and gravestones for generations.

Pictured is an unassuming home in Williamsburg during Lent. Note the purple fabric draped over the cross in the first-floor window and the statues in the second-floor window.

Here is a close-up of the saint statues in the previous photograph. From left to right are Our Lady of Fatima, the Sacred Heart of Jesus, and SS. Joseph, Rita of Cascia, Anthony, and Christopher.

Caffe Capri, also along Graham Avenue, has been offering espressos to locals and visitors to the Williamsburg Italian neighborhood for decades. Acting as a neighborhood hub for decades, the shop was unique in that its owners made a iced coffee that is fed through their gelato machine.

At the annual feast of Our Lady of Mount Carmel in East Williamsburg, the food attracts people from all over the country, not just New York City. Italian sausage and peppers, pork braciola, fried calamari, and zeppole are just some of the delicacies one can find here.

Here is a look down North Eighth Street, also known as Padre Pio Way, as the feast of Our Lady of Mount Carmel is in full swing. The bright lights, sounds, and aromas tantalize the senses.

Watching passersby from his front stoop, this gentleman in East Williamsburg's Italian neighborhood happily obliges to a photograph.

Pictured is the San Paolino statue outside of the Shrine Church of Our Lady of Mount Carmel in Williamsburg, Brooklyn. Family members of departed parishioners keep small signs in front of the statue for their intentions.

In addition to the dancing of the multistory adult Giglio, Williamsburg conducts a children's Dance of the Giglio, during which boys and girls have an opportunity to lift a smaller version of the Giglio in honor of San Paolino in exchange for blessings and graces. The only one of its kind in the United States, replicated from the adult Dance of the Giglio, is a practice stemming back hundreds of years to the town of Nola in Naples, Italy. A total of 60 children lift a 20-foot-tall tower to honor the town's patron saint, San Paolino, a bishop who offered himself in exchange for the release of young townsfolk who were taken as prisoners by the Ottomans.

Bamonte's Restaurant, featured here, is a Williamsburg fixture and one of the oldest Italian restaurants in the United States. Famed for its authenticity in Southern Italian fare, Bamonte's draws crowds from near and far.

On the first night of the feast of Our Lady of Mount Carmel, a procession takes place from the Shrine Church of Our Lady of Mount Carmel, and the Giglio Band leads the way, playing Italian folk songs from Naples.

The Our Lady of Mount Carmel statue is ushered out of the Shrine Church in Williamsburg to a volley of devotees shooting confetti and the Giglio Band gracing her presence at the beginning of the mile-long procession.

Pictured at left, devotees and members of the St. Paulinus Society proudly walk through the streets of Williamsburg behind their banner. The photograph at right depicts the Giglio with San Paolino all the way at the top and the Giglio Band and the monsignor of Our Lady of Mount Carmel at the base. Building this multistory structure takes weeks. It is a lost art that was brought over from Naples, specifically the town of Nola.

Here is a close look at the Giglio Band as it performs for attendees. They are playing atop the beams being carried on the shoulders of Giglio Boys of Williamsburg.

Carrying tons of weight, the Giglio Boys bob and weave and lift the Giglio to make it seem like San Paolino is dancing in an amazing choreography of sheer devotion and passion.

Three

THE ITALIAN SECTIONS
OF QUEENS

In the Bronx, there is a dense Little Italy that is centered upon Arthur Avenue. Catania Pizzeria marks one corner of this Little Italy's boundaries.

A neighborhood mainstay and one of the most well-known Italian eateries in New York City, Pasquale's Rigoletto still proudly serves delicious dishes to tourists and Italians from all over the city.

Side-by-side, Calandra Cheese and DeCicco Brothers Novelties are in good company with one another. Boasting "all types of homemade & imported" cheese, Calandra is well renowned in gourmet food circles.

This stoic photograph of Biancardi's classic storefront window does the talking for the most part. A butcher shop with authentic delicacies, such as tripe and rabbit, it is a favorite of Italians all throughout the borough as well as other parts of New York.

D' Bari Funeral Home, along Arthur Avenue, is where most residents from this community have had their final goodbyes with family members. Funerals and wakes are important ceremonies to most people in Italian neighborhoods in the five boroughs.

This "Welcome to Little Italy" sign marks another border of Little Italy at the foot of Arthur Avenue.

This beautiful shrine, located on a balcony overlooking a side street just off Arthur Avenue, pays homage to the Blessed Mother and the Sacred Heart of Jesus.

Even apartment buildings in Bronx's Little Italy show their Italian pride with an Italian flag proudly waving and a green, white, and red fire hydrant.

Pictured is Our Lady of Mount Carmel Church in the Bronx neighborhood known as either Belmont or Little Italy. The church is on East 187th Street.

Located in the Bronx's Little Italy, this signage along the Arthur Avenue side of Artuso Pastry Shop showcases vintage photographs that depict the bakery's past owners and the original storefront, which evoke a sense of nostalgia.

Fiorella LaGuardia urged the opening of the Arthur Avenue open-air retail market. In an effort to sanitize New York immigrant neighborhoods by ushering out pushcarts and street vendors, this open-air market is still in business and as successful as ever. Delicacies of all kinds as well as novelties and even hand-rolled cigars can be found inside.

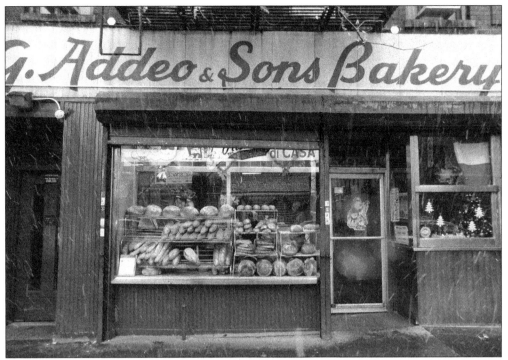

This snowy scene in Belmont depicts a great way to warm up with freshly baked bread from G. Addeo & Sons Bakery. The bakery offers some of the best breads and cookies in the five boroughs.

Here is a look inside of Calandra Cheese on Arthur Avenue. Samples of the mouthwatering cheeses from all over Italy and elsewhere are available for patrons to taste.

Pictured is the famous sausage chandelier in the Calabria Pork Store on Arthur Avenue. Patrons travel from all over the world to take photographs underneath the hundreds of cured Italian sausage.

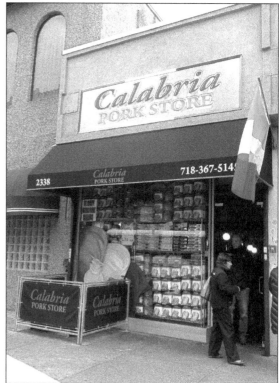

Here is the outside of the Calabria Pork Store on Arthur Avenue around Christmastime. The line from inside the store ends at the door.

Tony's Barber Shop at 597 East 187th Street is a classic barbershop and solidifies the Italian barbershop mystique.

In preparation for the feast of Sant' Antonio, 187th Street's Our Lady of Mount Carmel Church, pictured at left, is decorated accordingly. The Bronx has been home to many Italian neighborhoods. One neighborhood, along a three-block strip called Villa Avenue, has long since been Italian; however, some things, such as this old St. Anthony's clubhouse sign (right), still remain.

Teitel Brothers, established in 1915, is an Arthur Avenue institution that earned respect by serving food free of cost to neighborhood residents during the Great Depression.

This is a photograph of the outside of the Arthur Avenue Retail Market. The open-air market was created by Mayor Fiorello La Guardia in the mid-1930s to replace the pushcarts that were once there.

Pictured is one of the many retail shops inside the Arthur Avenue Retail Market. One can find pastries and coffee as well as focaccia and cheeses here.

Pictured at left is the heart of Villa Avenue's Italian neighborhood, St. Philip Neri Church. From this church, a St. Anthony statue was processed throughout the neighborhood for a feast that would draw crowds of thousands. At one end of Villa Avenue in the Grand Concourse section of the Bronx, a sign from moons ago is still hanging on the side of a building; it reads, "Jerry's Steak House," which was a local family restaurant.

Another Belmont establishment in Bronx's famed Little Italy is Terranova Bakery.

Here, Joe's Italian Deli displays cured prosciutto and cheeses, such as fresh burrata. It is a long-lasting Italian American institution in Bronx's Little Italy.

Four

THE BRONX'S
FAMED LITTLE ITALY
AND VILLA AVENUE

Holding an image of the Blessed Mother and Infant Jesus, devotees walk through the streets of the predominantly Italian neighborhood of Whitestone in honor of the Madonna dell'Arco.

Devotees and parishioners gather to celebrate the Madonna dell'Arco with food and drink in their Sunday best.

The Societa Concordia Partanna in Whitestone, a mutual aid society, was formed to provide benefits and support to family members arriving from Italy.

Members of the Societa Concordia Partanna in Whitestone are seen outside their club as the procession of Maria SS. Delle Grazie di Montevago makes its way through their neighborhood.

The procession of Maria SS. Delle Grazie di Montevago moves through the streets of Whitestone, a small little-known Italian enclave in Queens.

Corona, Queens, has been home to a large Italian community. This neighborhood's famous Lemon Ice King of Corona has been featured on the Food Network and is in the opening scene of *The King of Queens* television show. People come from all over to try its delicious Italian ices.

A bocce court, with the tricolor Italian flag painted alongside it, sits conveniently in the middle of Macaroni Park, located in the center of Corona.

This famous Italian eatery in Corona is called Parkside. Serving some of the best Italian food in the five boroughs, this authentic eatery has been the talk of the town in New York City for decades.

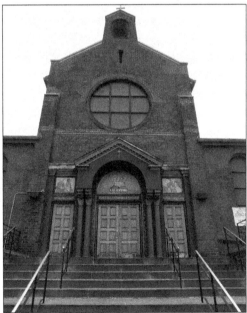

Corona is also home to Coppola-Migliore Funeral Home on 104th Street, pictured at left. As echoed previously, Italian-owned funeral homes have a very important role in providing neighborhood families an opportunity to grieve alongside loved ones and familiar faces. At right, St. Leo's Church, a territorial parish adopted by the Italian community, for decades has been the center of this Italian neighborhood. Masses are still held in Italian.

Mama's Backyard Café, a food phenomenon, was the favorite spot of the New York Mets, so another shop was opened at Citi Field. Owned and operated by the same family for decades, the mozzarella is homemade and some of the best in the five boroughs.

Astoria, Queens, has a significant Italian population. Immaculate Conception, located on Twenty-ninth Street and Ditmars Boulevard, is the heart of the Italian community in Astoria.

A look at the Mass schedule of Immaculate Conception church tells of the Italian parishioner base by virtue of the Italian Mass.

An Astoria fixture, the Dave and Tony Salumeria shop has been making fresh mozzarella and Italian delicacies for decades.

This beautiful Blessed Mother statue is underneath an arch of flowers in front of a home in Astoria, Queens.

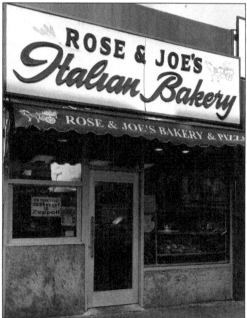

The Sant' Antonio Abate Castrofillipo Fraternal Society on Ditmars Boulevard in Astoria is home to the neighborhood's devotees of St. Anthony. Inside the club, there is a fine statue of the saint that is processed each year. Rare Italian pastries, such as St. Joseph's sfingi and zeppole, can be found alongside some of the best Italian bread in Queens at Rose and Joe's Italian Bakery. Note the Sicilian cart and donkey on the sign.

A fine purveyor of Italian delicacies and homemade sausage, Rosario's is another fixture and magnet for foodies in Astoria, Queens. Note the gentleman sporting his Italian pride as he leisurely strolls along the street.

Although up there in years, this ornate St. Jude statue still beautifully represents this resident's devotion.

Even though New York has no shortage of good Italian bakeries, there are not many that have been around as long as La Guli, which has been in business since 1937.

Parisi Bakery is yet another long-standing Italian bakery in Astoria, Queens.

The facade of the San Rocco Society of Astoria's clubhouse reads, "Viva San Rocco," in green, white, and red. "Live St. Rocco" is the English translation.

This family in Astoria has had the statuary for Our Lady of Mount Carmel built into the front side of their home.

This street in Corona, in front of St. Leo Church, is named after resident Edward F. Guida Sr. He was the owner of Guida Funeral Home on 104th Street.

The front of Mama's Backyard Café in Corona, Queens, exhibits collages of family and customer photographs, which are held dear to the neighborhood's collective heart.

Mama's Backyard Café has a classic interior replete with a vintage display case and cured sausage.

Another members-only society in Astoria is the Fraternal Society of Canicatti. These societies were the backbone of Italian communities when benefits and insurances were not available to Italian immigrants.

The feast of Madonna dell'Arco is about to begin as devotees pose for a photograph with the exquisitely ornate painting of La Madonna and Infant Jesus in Whitestone, Queens.

Devotees decorate the statue of the Madonna Delle Grazie inside their church.

Carrying the candelabra atop one's head is an ancient practice, attributed to Southern Italian processions, and this woman shows her devotion in this extraordinary feat in Whitestone, Queens.

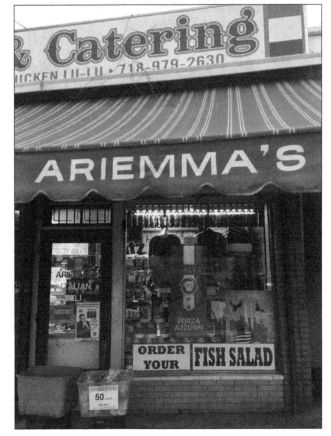

Staten Island is home to more Italians than any other borough. As seen here, Ariemma's, a pork store that has been on the island for decades, not only sells homemade Italian delicacies, but also souvenirs to meet the demand for Italian pride.

Pastosa Ravioli also has a location along Richmond Road in Staten Island's Dongan Hills neighborhood. This area still has many Italians living in it as evidenced by Pastosa's thriving business.

Situated along Hylan Boulevard, Bruno's Bakery and Restaurant (seen at left) is home to delicious desserts and a wonderful atmosphere in Dongan Hills. First founded in Manhattan, two brothers wound up spreading the love by popular demand to the borough of Staten Island as many people from Manhattan also moved to the borough after the construction of the Verrazzano Bridge. Pictured at right is the Moretti Bakery, the oldest Italian bakery on Staten Island. Started over four decades ago, this Italian bakery draws crowds from all over the borough.

Our Lady of Mount Carmel Grotto in Staten Island is a shrine for the Blessed Virgin Mary. People come from all over the tristate area to worship here.

Here is another look at Our Lady of Mount Carmel Grotto in Staten Island.

Residents walk throughout the shrine to pray and light votive candles for loved ones or for prayer intentions concerning the deceased or sick.

Pictured at left, a gentleman sits inside the grotto among the many saint statues and votive candles. The St. Anthony statue, pictured at right, shows its age but still exudes beauty and devotion. Italian sculptors crafted it for the Alba House Wayside Shrine. The Alba House is a religious bookstore on Staten Island.

About the
Italian Enclaves
Historical Society

Founded by author Raymond Guarini in March 2019, the Italian Enclaves Historical Society serves to catalogue and document every Italian neighborhood or enclave that has existed in the United States since the Italian diaspora in the 19th century; to say the least, it is a monumental task. Guarini has curated a board of directors comprised of like-minded individuals intent upon preserving Italian American culture from different parts of the country. A Brooklyn native, Guarini has spent the majority of his time documenting and researching within the five boroughs of Manhattan where the Italian Enclaves Historical Society maintains most of its current and historical content.

DISCOVER THOUSANDS OF LOCAL HISTORY BOOKS FEATURING MILLIONS OF VINTAGE IMAGES

Arcadia Publishing, the leading local history publisher in the United States, is committed to making history accessible and meaningful through publishing books that celebrate and preserve the heritage of America's people and places.

Find more books like this at
www.arcadiapublishing.com

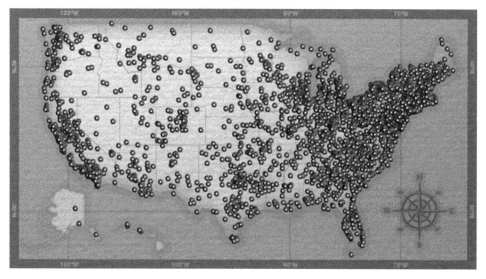

Search for your hometown history, your old
stomping grounds, and even your favorite sports team.

CPSIA information can be obtained
at www.ICGtesting.com
Printed in the USA
BVHW011017240721
612420BV00021B/585